First World War
and Army of Occupation
War Diary
France, Belgium and Germany

52 DIVISION
156 Infantry Brigade,
Brigade Trench Mortar Battery
1 April 1918 - 10 February 1919

WO95/2897/5

The Naval & Military Press Ltd
www.nmarchive.com
Published in association with The National Archives

Published by

The Naval & Military Press Ltd

Unit 10 Ridgewood Industrial Park,

Uckfield, East Sussex,

TN22 5QE England

Tel: +44 (0) 1825 749494

www.naval-military-press.com

www.nmarchive.com

This diary has been reprinted in facsimile from the original. Any imperfections are inevitably reproduced and the quality may fall short of modern type and cartographic standards.

© Crown Copyright
Images reproduced by permission of The National Archives, London, England, 2015.

Contents

Document type	Place/Title	Date From	Date To
Heading	WO95/2897-5		
Heading	52nd Division 156th Infy Bde 156th Lt. Trench Mortar Bty 1918 Apl-1919 Jan		
Heading	156th Brigade 52nd Division Battery Disembarked Marseilles From Egypt 17.4.18 156th Light Trench Mortar Battery April 1918		
Heading	War Diary Of 156th Bde Light Trench Mortar Battery 1st To 30th April 1918 Volume IX		
War Diary	Surafend	01/04/1918	03/04/1918
War Diary	Kantara	04/04/1918	05/04/1918
War Diary	Alexandria	06/04/1918	10/04/1918
War Diary	At Sea	11/04/1918	16/04/1918
War Diary	Marseilles	17/04/1918	21/04/1918
War Diary	St Firmin	22/04/1918	25/04/1918
War Diary	Halines	26/04/1918	26/04/1918
War Diary	Mametz	27/04/1918	27/04/1918
War Diary	Glominghem	28/04/1918	30/04/1918
Miscellaneous	To D.A.G 3rd Echelon	06/05/1918	06/05/1918
Heading	War Diary Of 156th Trench Mortar Battery 1st To 31st May 1918 Volume X		
War Diary	Glominghem	01/05/1918	08/05/1918
War Diary	Neuville St Vaast	09/05/1918	31/05/1918
Heading	War Diary Of 156th Trench Mortar Battery 1st To 30th June 1918 Volume XI		
War Diary	In The Line Batty H.Q. A.5.d 4.6 Maroeuil 1/20000	01/06/1918	03/06/1918
War Diary	Neuville St Vaast	04/06/1918	11/06/1918
War Diary	Batty H.Q. T13.d.5.7 Maroeuil 1/20000	12/06/1918	12/06/1918
War Diary	T.13d 5.7 Maroeuil 1/20000	12/06/1918	30/06/1918
Heading	War Diary Of 156th Trench Mortar Battery 1st To 31st July 1918 Volume XII		
War Diary	Hanson Camp Neuville St Vaast	01/07/1918	22/07/1918
Miscellaneous	156th Trench Mortar Battery Training Programme	25/07/1918	25/07/1918
War Diary	Bois D'Olhain	22/07/1918	31/07/1918
War Diary	Battery H.Qrs B.26.b.7.2 Bailleul (2nd Edition) 1/20000	31/07/1918	31/07/1918
Heading	War Diary Of 156th Trench Mortar Battery 1st To 31st August 1918 Volume XIII		
War Diary	Battery H.Qrs B.26.b.7.2 Bailleul (2nd Edtn) 1/20,000	01/08/1918	16/08/1918
War Diary	Berles	17/08/1918	20/08/1918
War Diary	Berneville	21/08/1918	22/08/1918
War Diary	Blaireville	23/08/1918	24/08/1918
War Diary	France Edition 8d Local Sheet 51b SW 1/20,000	24/08/1918	28/08/1918
War Diary	M35 C.27	29/08/1918	31/08/1918
War Diary	U 7 A.8.3	31/08/1918	31/08/1918
War Diary	France Edition 8 (d) Local sheet 56 S.W 1/20,000	31/08/1918	31/08/1918
Heading	War Diary Of 156th Trench Mortar Battery 1st To 30th September 1918 Volume XIV		
War Diary	Battery Hqrs U 7 A 8.4 Sheet 51b SW France Edition 8d (Local) 1/20,000	01/09/1918	02/09/1918
War Diary	U 14 C 7.1	03/09/1918	03/09/1918
War Diary	U 30 D	04/09/1918	06/09/1918

War Diary	St Ledger	07/09/1918	16/09/1918
War Diary	D 1 A.2.5	17/09/1918	19/09/1918
War Diary	D 15	20/09/1918	20/09/1918
War Diary	Hqrs E 19.a.8.8	21/09/1918	26/09/1918
War Diary	D.30 B 1-4	27/09/1918	30/09/1918
Heading	War Diary Of 156th Trench Mortar Battery 1st To 31st October 1918 Volume XV		
War Diary	Battery Hqrs L.3 C.1.7 Sheet 57c NE	01/10/1918	07/10/1918
War Diary	Izel-Les-Hameaux	08/10/1918	20/10/1918
War Diary	Auby Q33 A 4.3 Sheet 44a	21/10/1918	23/10/1918
War Diary	Auby	24/10/1918	24/10/1918
War Diary	Coutiches M 2 D 2.3 Sheet 44	25/10/1918	27/10/1918
War Diary	Lacelles	27/10/1918	28/10/1918
War Diary	J33 A9.9 Sheet 44 1/40,000	29/10/1918	31/10/1918
Heading	War Diary Of 156th Trench Mortar Battery 1st To 31st December 1918 Volume XVII		
War Diary	Thoricourt	01/12/1918	16/12/1918
War Diary	Hubermont	17/12/1918	31/12/1918
Miscellaneous	156th Trench Mortar Battery Training Programme	14/12/1918	14/12/1918
Miscellaneous	156th Trench Mortar Battery Training Programme	21/12/1918	21/12/1918
Miscellaneous	156th Trench Mortar Battery Training Programme	28/12/1918	28/12/1918
Miscellaneous	156th Trench Mortar Battery Training Programme	04/01/1919	04/01/1919
Heading	War Diary Of 156th Trench Mortar Battery 1st To 31st January 1919 Volume XVIII		
War Diary	Hubermont	01/01/1919	31/01/1919
Heading	War Diary Of The 156th Trench Mortar Battery 1st To 10th February 1919 Volume XIX		
War Diary	Hubermont	01/02/1919	10/02/1919

3005/28975(s)

3007/28975(s)

52ND DIVISION
156TH INFY BDE

156TH LT. TRENCH MORTAR BTY

~~APR - DEC 1918~~

1918 APL — 1919 JAN

156th Brigade.
52nd Division.

Battery disembarked MARSEILLES from EGYPT 17.4.18.

156th LIGHT TRENCH MORTAR BATTERY

APRIL 1918.

WAR DIARY
or
INTELLIGENCE SUMMARY.
(Erase heading not required.)

Army Form C. 2118.

Original

War Diary
of
152nd Bde Light Trench Mortar Battery
1st to 30th April 1918

Volume IX

Army Form C. 2118.

WAR DIARY
or
INTELLIGENCE SUMMARY.
(Erase heading not required.)

96th Bde. R.G.A. Battery

Instructions regarding War Diaries and Intelligence Summaries are contained in F. S. Regs., Part II. and the Staff Manual respectively. Title pages will be prepared in manuscript.

Place	Date	Hour	Summary of Events and Information	Remarks and references to Appendices
Surafend	1/4/18		In Bivouac area. Ordnance stores, except guns & working utensils returned to A.O.D. Dumps at Surafend.	1/4/18
"	2/4/18		Battery transport returned to Advance Remount Depot, Kura	2/4/18
"	3/4/18		Moved from Surafend at 1400 entrained at Ludd for Kantara East	3/4/18
"			Arrived at Kantara East at 1000 & marched to No 14 of Base Depot. 1 O.R. to hospital	3/4/18
Kantara	4/4/18			4/4/18
"	5/4/18		Moved from Kantara East at 0100 & entrained at Kantara West for Alexandria. Arrived at Alexandria at 1300 embarked on H.M.T. Kashmir.	5/4/18
Alexandria	6/4/18		On board HMT Kashmir, lying in dock	6/4/18
	7/4/18		do	7/4/18
	8/4/18		do	8/4/18

Army Form C. 2118.

WAR DIARY
or
INTELLIGENCE SUMMARY.
(Erase heading not required.)

Place	Date	Hour	Summary of Events and Information	Remarks and references to Appendices
Alexandria	9/4/18		On board H.M.T. Kanowna lying in dock	
"	10/4/18		do	
At Sea	11/4/18		Sailed at 14.00. Battery to provide permanent crews for ships guns during the voyage. 3 - 76.60 & 9 m.m.	
"	12/4/18		At Sea. Six other ships with convoy escorted by Japanese D.B. Ds	
"	13/4/18		at Sea	
"	14/4/18		do	
"	15/4/18		do	
"	16/4/18		do	
Marseilles	17/4/18		Arrived at Marseilles at 9 a.m. D.M. Battery & M.B. coy remaining on board overnight.	

Army Form C. 2118.

WAR DIARY
or
INTELLIGENCE SUMMARY.
(Erase heading not required.)

Instructions regarding War Diaries and Intelligence Summaries are contained in F. S. Regs., Part II. and the Staff Manual respectively. Title pages will be prepared in manuscript.

Place	Date	Hour	Summary of Events and Information	Remarks and references to Appendices
Marseilles	18/4/16		Entrained at Marseilles at 8 am. Dress four marching order.	
	19/4/16		On train.	
	20/4/16		do	
	21/4/16		Arrived at Nogales marched to billets at St Jennin.	
St Jennin	22/4/16		Cleaning kits etc. C.O. to Lahtar	
	23/4/16		Gas drill, close order drill. Musketry. Route march. Lecture Course of Drill uniform	
	24/4/16	3. O & 8.	C.O. to Lahtar. Gun mounting staging mounting 55 Ko. work by Gas drill. Lecture musics of Gun team. Officers MO Re equivalent to principal Bank, at Lec for shipment to UK.	

WAR DIARY
or
INTELLIGENCE SUMMARY.

(Erase heading not required.)

Army Form C. 2118.

Instructions regarding War Diaries and Intelligence Summaries are contained in F.S. Regs., Part II. and the Staff Manual respectively. Title pages will be prepared in manuscript.

2nd Bn. L. N. Battery

Place	Date	Hour	Summary of Events and Information	Remarks and references to Appendices
St Germain	2/4/18		Marched to Gun & entrained for Abbeyene. Arrived at Abbeyene 24/8/18	J.M.M
			2/m marched to Buick at Halevis	
Halevis	25/4/18		Moved from Halevis to Julien in infantry all cavalries returned to U.K.	J.M.M
Julien	27/4/18		Moved into huts at Blangington	J.M.M
Blangington	28/4/18		Losing huts etc	J.M.M
	29/4/18		Gas drill. Lt Heron & 64 O.R's passed gas hut (Chevron, Lachnamoy, Jones) Captn J. Shaw, Palmer & 190 Royal Scots attached for rail, Capth J. Cox took over command of Battery	J.M.M
	30/4/18		Gas drill, musketry & Lewis mortar & bayonet fighting. Battery retained duties in bayonet fighting to be complete OR returned otherwise	J.M.M

WAR DIARY
INTELLIGENCE SUMMARY

Army Form C. 2118.

156 Bde L.T.M. Battery

Place	Date	Hour	Summary of Events and Information	Remarks and references to Appendices
Gouvigny	30/4/18		Personnel of Battery at this date, 4 Officers & 70 other ranks.	30/4/18

Officers
3   7th Royal Scots
1   4th do
—   6th Scottish Rifles
—
4

Other Ranks
16   4th Royal Scots
21   7th do
12   7th Scottish Rifles
21   8th do
—
70

Ja Law Capt
OC 156th Brigade
L.T.M. Battery

To D.A.G.
  3rd Echelon
   B.E.F.
    France

Herewith War Diary of 156th
Trench Mortar Battery for April 1918

　　　　　　　　　J. Stott
　　　　　　　　　　　　Capt
　　　　　　　O/c 156th T.M. Batty

In the field
6/5/18

Army Form C. 2118

WAR DIARY
or
INTELLIGENCE SUMMARY

(Erase heading not required.)

Confidential

Original

War Diary
of
156th Trench Mortar Battery

1st to 31st May, 1918.

Volume X.

156 Bde. L.T.M. Battery

WAR DIARY
or
INTELLIGENCE SUMMARY.

Army Form C. 2118.

Page 1.

Place	Date	Hour	Summary of Events and Information	Remarks and references to Appendices
Sevenoaks	1/5/18		Battery training carried out according to programme. 2 O.Rs to hospital	A.1.3
"	2/5/18		Carried out training according to programme.	A.1.3
"	3/5/18		Parade as usual. 4 Batty marched to attend gas demonstration	6.1.1.3
"	4/5/18		Lieut G.G. Batters arrived. Batters attached to Battery. 4 O.Rs returned their work. 1 O.R. proceeded on leave to U.K.	2.1.1.3
			2/Lt. A.W.B. Wilson attached to Battery.	
"	5/5/18		61 O.R. attached to Battery. 2 O.R. admitted to hospital and 1 O.R. proceeded on leave to U.K. Battery ordered to Syllabus by G.G. Batters.	8.1.1.3
"	6/5/18		Divine service carried out.	3.1.1.1
"	7/5/18		To Neuville St Vaast as party for firing point. Parade according to Syllabus.	
"	8/5/18		Parade according to Syllabus. Battery paraded and 1 O.R. detailed for duty. 2/Lt. A.W.B. Wilson attended a class in Bayonet fighting	2.1.1.3
			On Fielding.	
Neuville St Vaast	9/5/18	2 A.M. 6-10 P.M.	Battery entrained at 6.10 P.M. to proceed to new area. Arrived new area 2 A.M. attached officers and O.Rs joined Battery.	A.1.3 A.1.3 A.1.3
"	10/5/18		Battery reorganised.	
"	11/5/18		Parade as per Syllabus. Battery paraded for Batt.	
"	12/5/18		Parade as per Syllabus. Battery paraded for musketry course at Nortemplore.	2.1.1.3
"	13/5/18		Parade as per Syllabus. 4 O.Rs rejoined their work. 1 O.R. hosp.	8.1.1.3
"	14/5/18		2/Lt. A.W.B. Turner + 2/Lt. A.B. Wilson together with 38 O.Rs rejoined their unit. 1 O.R. hosp.	10.1.1.3
			3 O.R. proceeded on their leave to U.K. Battery marched to Hornets Change. 2/Lt. G.G. groups and refreshers practices were carried out.	2.1.1.3
"	15/5/18		Battery attached on Field Battery. 2/Lt. G.G. Smith and 1 O.R. proceeded on 14 days leave to U.K.	A.10.1
			1 O.R. to hospital.	

156 Bde T.M.B.

Army Form C. 2118

WAR DIARY or INTELLIGENCE SUMMARY
(Erase heading not required.)

Page 2.

Place	Date	Hour	Summary of Events and Information	Remarks and references to Appendices
Neuville St Vaast	10/5/16		Parade as per syllabus. Battery paraded 2 P.M. and proceeded to trenches and took over from 154 Bde L.T.M.B. 6 guns in line where co-ordinates are as follows. No 1 Gun T.28.c.8.8. } Right Sect. No 2 " B.4.c.4.1. No 5 " T.28.a.8.0 } under 2/Lt. M.J. Gyling. No 3 " B.4.c.6.4. No 6 " T.22.d.9.3. } middle St Sanneville No 5 " B.4.c.5.8.	
	14/5/16		Battery H.Q. at A.5.d.4.6. Baft. staff MAROEUIL 1/20,000 Baft. Staff visited pits in life. Enemy shelled. Passed over our lines at 11 A.M. being heavily shelled to our Anti-aircraft guns. Our aeroplanes very active all day. Situation unchanged. Completed nightly fatigue carried out. Bomb. dropped and replaced behind Enemy lines. Lt. L.W. Smith worked pits in line. I.O.R. proceeded on 14 days leave to U.K. Very little activity.	
	19/5/16			
	18/5/16		Lt. Ildeave with reserve 2 guns took up new position. Guns being known as A and B, co-ordinates Jupshali are as follows: A gun at B.10.a.7.8. } fly staff MAROEUIL 1/20,000 B " at B.10.a.7.10. } Enemy artillery very active in Right Sector. B.4.W.A.H.	
	19/5/16		Work done on new line. Enemy artillery fairly quiet.	
	20/5/16		Verified pits in line. Bafts staff visited pits in line.	
	21/5/16		B Det. partially filled in to hostile shell (direct hit).	
	22/5/16		Work done on reserve position and cleaning arm. Enemy's forward position shelled by our heavies. Our plane brought down by enemy A.A. Bailey finally 5 rounds on Communication trenches. Situation unchanged each man to U.K. 10 R. H. Shaf S.A.A. rounds to machine received. I.O.R. proceeded on 14 days leave to U.K.	
	23/5/16		Position shelled and Ammn cleared. Very little artillery activity. I.O.R. proceeded on 14 days leave to U.K. Bombers detailed to attend course at G.H.Q. Bomb. School shown in Rifle Bombers. ranks arrived at Army position on 24 inst. All	

1875   Wt. W593/826   1,000,000   4/15   J.B.C. & A.   A.D.S.S./Forms/C. 2118.

WAR DIARY
or
INTELLIGENCE SUMMARY
(Erase heading not required.)

Army Form C. 2118

156 Bde. T.M.B.

Page 3

Place	Date	Hour	Summary of Events and Information	Remarks and references to Appendices
	24/5/16		Blaming shells and ??? ??? ??? left battled with. Battery practice carried out as normal. Artillery activity normal. O.R. proceeded 14 days leave to U.K. of practice carried out as normal.	A.4/1
	25/5/16		Guns to increase constructed. Ammn. shelved and slab from ... I.O.R. to U.K. on 14 days leave. Artillery activity normal.	A.4/3
	26/5/16		Blaming shells and ??? ???. 4 recesses entered. Battery actively normal. 1 O.R. proceeded 14 days leave to U.K. 1 O.R. returned U.K. on 14 weeks leave (Class expired)	A.4/A
	27/5/16		1 O.R. to hospital from gun practice camp at ??. 1 O.R. reported back from San Bernard at Giovani. Battery ??? practice carried out.	A.V.A.
	28/5/16		At 3 a.m. No. 1 Howitzer fired by ?? ??? ??? 2 ??? two ???. The Howitzer kept a constant ??? — Battery firing practice carried out. Investigated the ???? the ???? a constant ???? — ??? activity normal.	??
	29/5/16		I.O.R. to hospital. Source of ammunition supply in ??? 2 ???. — Field Ambulance. — Repair of ??? commenced. N.C.I.O.R. inspected & ammunition replenished. Battery firing practice carried out. Battery activity normal. 2 ??? ??? fired in reserve ??? line.	??
	30/5/16		Mobile reserve takes ammunition replenished. Battery fired ??? S.O.S. Battery artillery carried out.	??
	31/5/16		H 9 a.m. shoot proceeded to M. Lalin. Practiced 1st Battery into two district of 9,000. Same for following day. 1st S.O.S. cannot meet at 9.30 am. No.1, 2, 3, & 4's guns were attached to ??? firing practice carried out ??? ??? at ?? down. It of our shot expected about 112 m.	??
			M.C. & Scouts returned to Field Ambulance. No. ??? two men again at ?? ??? General artillery activity. Battery firing practice carried out. ??? ??? ???	??

??? ?????
3 - 1/7 Royal Scots
1 - 1/7 Royal Scots
??? - 1/8 ??? Rifles

18 - 1/4 Royal Scots
26 - 1/7 ??
20 - 1/7 ??
33 - 1/8 Scottish Rifles

J. Scott Col.
OC 156 T.M. Batty

Army Form C. 2118.

Original

WAR DIARY
or
INTELLIGENCE SUMMARY.
(Erase heading not required.)

Confidential.

War Diary
of
156th Trench Mortar Battery.

1st to 30th June, 1918.

Volume XI

Army Form C. 2118

WAR DIARY
or
INTELLIGENCE SUMMARY
(Erase heading not required.)

156. T.M. Battery.

Instructions regarding War Diaries and Intelligence Summaries are contained in F.S. Regs., Part II. and the Staff Manual respectively. Title Pages will be prepared in manuscript.

Place	Date	Hour	Summary of Events and Information	Remarks and references to Appendices
In the Line Battery H.Q. As d & b Newport France	1/6/18		Personnel of Battery at this date Officers 3 1/7 Royal Scots 1 1/7 " " 1 4/7 Scottish Rifles 1 1/8 " " Men 18 1/7 Royal Scots 24 1/7 " " 26 4/7 Scottish Rifles 23 1/8 " "	
	2/6/18		Lt. E. T. Smith & O.R. reported from leave in U.K.	
	3/6/18	9 a.m.	1 Offr & about 40 O.R.s attended 157 T.M. Battery & proceeded to Rifle Range Neuville St. Vaast.	
	4/6/18	2 p.m.	Bn. proceeded to Battn. scheme of 30/5/18 from here in C.T. Formed up for Programme. Officers attended lecture on Trench Mortars at Div. Camp Schm.	
Newville St Vaast	5/6/18		Carrying on for Programme. Firing with Dummies. 1 Offr & O.R.s on Last.	
	7/6/18		Lieut. Shane with 4/8 Scottish Rifles Lewis Gun Coy. detailed as members of Court. Carrying on for Programme.	
	8/6/18		Grew used in mounting Barrage in Counter Attack of L.G.Cs. to execute at Lent Camp 8th June 1918.	

1875 Wt. W593/826 1,000,000 4/15 J.B.C.&A. A.D.S.S./Forms/C. 2118.

156 T.M. Batty

Instructions regarding War Diaries and Intelligence Summaries are contained in F. S. Regs., Part II. and the Staff Manual respectively. Title Pages will be prepared in manuscript.

WAR DIARY
or
INTELLIGENCE SUMMARY
(Erase heading not required.)

Army Form C. 2118

Place	Date	Hour	Summary of Events and Information	Remarks and references to Appendices
Neuville St Vaast	9/6/18		Divine Service at Y.M.C.A. Hut at Neuville St Vaast. Captain Scott attended conference at Brigade H.Q. St Eloy. Congratulatory message sent to B.G.C. on his being decorated with C.M.G. & message of thanks received. 2 O/Rs reported from U.K. Leave.	nil
			2/Lt A.W. Smith struck off effective strength as from this date.	nil
	10/6/18		Captain Scott & Lt E.T. Smith went over Left Sector of Line at present held by 155 Inf Bde. Training as per programme.	nil
	11/6/18		Training as per programme. Men paraded for Baths. 2/Lts W. Summersby & R.T. Ogilvy went round Left Sector of Line taking with them 4 O/Rs who were left in line as Advance Party.	nil
Batty H.Q. T13 d.5.7 MARDEUIL Sheet	12/6/18		Battery relieved 155 T.M. Batty in Left Sector of line. Six guns in line, two in support at Batty H.Q.	nil
			Disposition of Guns etc	
			Right Section Guns Nos 1, 2 & 3 Near Brunswick Tr & Freddie Gerrard Tr	nil
			Left Section Guns Nos 4, 5 & 6 Poppie Tr & Keane Tr	nil
			Batty H.Q. T13 d.5.7 MARDEUIL 1/20000 to 3.5.17	
			Ammunition in line taken over very excessive, about 8,000 shells. Gun Pits very unsatisfactory, three of them practically in the open. Improvement of same commenced. Slight hostile Artillery fire.	nil

1875 Wt. W593/826 1,000,000 4/15 J.B.C. & A. A.D.S.S./Forms/C. 2118.

Army Form C. 2118.

WAR DIARY
or
INTELLIGENCE SUMMARY.
(Erase heading not required.)

15-C. T.M. Battery

Instructions regarding War Diaries and Intelligence Summaries are contained in F. S. Regs., Part II. and the Staff Manual respectively. Title pages will be prepared in manuscript.

Place	Date	Hour	Summary of Events and Information	Remarks and references to Appendices
T.13.d.6.7. M, 20E.12 4 p.m.	2/4/15		3570 reported from L/C Crowe at 8/7M increased on O.K. crane	ack
	3/4/15		L/Cpl Crowe at etaples	ack
			L/Cpl Awdel evacuated to etaples influenza	ack
			shot for 2 days by 25089 Pte John Ingham epilepsy	ack
			Information received which we believe reliable that Ingham	ack
			Improvement of shells. Some hostile	ack
		4/4/15	Shelling into Reilly fine the	ack
	5/4/15		L/Cpl Crouch stood off allowed shoot for	ack
			Relief on enemy has been quiet	ack
			L/Cpl Crouch moved to old but sub Lieutenant evacuated	ack
			L/Cpl Thomas at duty Illness improvement of shells continued	ack
		6/4/15	L/Cpl to Lister Ambulance sent L/Cpl Cannell with duck de—	ack
	7/4/15		L/Cpl Robinson from O.R Crane L/C Cannell at duty T.G.	ack
			recovered at duty T.G.	ack
	8/4/15		Visit from the building line in upon the duty help	ack
	9/4/15		L/Cpl Richer Lt. Cpl Nbl. 3728C Cpl Stannard Van 5 Sgt	ack
			taken relieved thought of Battery	ack

15-6 F.M. Artillery

WAR DIARY or INTELLIGENCE SUMMARY

Army Form C. 2118.

Place	Date	Hour	Summary of Events and Information	Remarks and references to Appendices
T.12.d.5.y MARRIEUL YPRES	20.6.18		1 O.R. to C.K. on leave. 1 O.R. attended for Gas Course at FRESSIN. Batteries in line carried out Improvement of Gun Pits.	assembly 23.6.18
	21.6.18		Carried out Ammunition.	
			1 O.R. admitted to Field Amb. Sick. New bunkers for Pers.	
			2nd Event completed Semi artillery fire on wagon of	
			Battery H.Q. M26594 Style j Kw Stand off Efficient strength	
			on being 3 days in Field Amb 2 offrs 2 other ranks	
	22.6.18		Two new Pits constructed & the enemy's Rear of Ammunition	
			in Forward dumps slack. Hostile artillery fire normal	
			Battey H.Q. - A.25. S.9. & Cent. Gas shells	
	23.6.18		fired in new pits & Ammunition carried on	
	24.6.18		1 O.R. to C.K. on leave	
	25.6.18		1 O.R. from Field Amb. 1 O.R. from Course in U.K. 2nd Lt	30.6.18
			S.D. Nash detailed to attend Gas Course at FRESSIN assembly	
	26.6.18		Sniping shells at Gun slopes Enough two about	
			Shelling in neighbourhood Battey H.R. & Shellbouer at Event Enough	

WAR DIARY
or
INTELLIGENCE SUMMARY.

(Erase heading not required.)

Army Form C. 2118.

156 T.M. Battery

Place	Date	Hour	Summary of Events and Information	Remarks and references to Appendices
T.13 d 5.7 MARŒUIL /20000	27.6.18		2nd Lt. E.D. Watson & Lt. Ellis of the 1/8 Bn. Rfl. returned off Attached strength of Battery on returning to their Unit for duty	ref
	28.6.18		1 Offr & O.R. on leave. Lt. Ellis struck off Attached strength on temp comd in lieu Cond.	ref ref
	29.6.18		1 Offr struck off Effective Strength on being admitted to hospital — wounded	ref
	30.6.18		Battery relieved in the line by 157 T.M. Batty & proceeded to harass camp Personnel of Battery at time date Officers Nil + Men	
			2 1/4 Royal Scots	
			16 1/5 Royal Scots	
			22 1/7 Royal Scots	
			29 1/4 Seaforth Rfls	
			12 1/8 Scottish Rfls	ref

O.C. Battery

Army Form C. 2118.
Original

WAR DIARY
or
INTELLIGENCE SUMMARY.
(Erase heading not required.)

Confidential.

War Diary
of
156th Trench Mortar Battery.

1st to 31st July, 1918.

Volume XII

WAR DIARY or INTELLIGENCE SUMMARY

156th T.M. Battery.

Army Form C. 2118.

Ref Map LENS 1/100,000

Sheet No. 1.

Place	Date	Hour	Summary of Events and Information	Remarks and references to Appendices
Aaron Camp, NEUVILLE ST VAAST.	1.7.18		Personnel of Battery at this date:— Officers:— Other Ranks. 2. 1/4th Royal Scots. 16. 1/4th Royal Scots. 1. 1/8th Scottish Rifles. 22. 1/7th Royal Scots. 19. 1/4th Scottish Rifles. 12. 1/8th Scottish Rifles.	
	"		1 O.R. proceeded on leave to U.K. Battery fired.	wt
	"		Day devoted to cleaning up, & parade to Baths.	wt
	2.7.18		1 O.R. proceeded on leave to U.K. & 1 O.R. returned from leave in U.K.	wt
	"		Physical Exercises, Musketry, Close Order Drill, & Handling of Arms.	wt
	"		1 O.R. struck off attached strength on returning to unit.	wt
	"		Pte. Kingshott promoted to L/Cpl on being appointed Tess corporal vice A/L/Cpl.	wt
	"		Dykes who reverts to private.	wt
	"		A/L/Cpl. Amit & Pte. Crichton promoted to rank of L/Cpl.	wt
	3.7.18		Physical Exercises, Musketry, Battery Drill.	wt
	"		Following personnel struck off attached strength on rejoining their units:— 6 O.Rs. 1/4th Royal Scots, 6 O.Rs. 1/7th Royal Scots, 8 O.Rs. 1/7th Sco. Rifles.	wt
	"		1 O.R. taken on effective strength.	wt

156th Tn. Battery.

WAR DIARY or INTELLIGENCE SUMMARY.

Army Form C. 2118.

Sheet No. 2

Place	Date	Hour	Summary of Events and Information	Remarks and references to Appendices
	4-4-18		Physical Exercises, Musketry, Battery Drill. 2 B.Rs. worn between 10 & 10.30 am. Lieut W. Somerville detailed as member of F.S.C.M. assembling at	
FORT GEORGE	5-4-18		2 B.Rs. worn between 10 & 10.30 am. Physical Exercises. Gas lect.	
at FORT GEORGE			Everyone in camp proceeded to Baths.	
	6-4-18		2 B.Rs. worn between 10 & 10.30 am. Physical Exercises, musketry, Close Order Drill, Handling of Guns.	
	"		1 O/R. admitted to Field Ambulance for Dental Treatment.	
	"		2 O/Rs. proceeded to First Army Rest Camp AUDRESSELLES.	
	7-4-18		1 O/R. taken on effective strength. 2 O/Rs. reported from leave in U.K.	
	8-4-18		Cleaning of Guns & Gun Drill. 1 O/R. returned from Field Ambulance. O/C Battery went round Right Sector of line, taking with him 9 O/Rs. who were left in line as Advance party.	
	"		1 Off. & 1 O/R. proceeded on leave to U.K. 2 O/Rs admitted to Field Ambulance for Dental Treatment	
	9-4-18		Battery relieved 155th Tn. Battery in Right Sector of line. 8 Guns in line.	

WAR DIARY
or
INTELLIGENCE SUMMARY

Army Form C. 2118.

156th T.M. Battery.

Sheet No. 3.

Place	Date	Hour	Summary of Events and Information	Remarks and references to Appendices
Battery H.Qrs. B.2.a.5.4. LA TARGETTE 1/20,000				
	11.7.18		1 O.R. reported from leave in U.K. 2 O.R. reported from Field Ambulance	
	13.7.18		1 O.R. reported from course at I.M. School, SAILLY-FLIBEAUCOURT.	
	15.7.18		3 Gun Detachments in WILLERVAL sector relieved by Detachments from 10th Can. T.M. Battery.	
	"		3 Gun positions taken over from 154th T.M. Battery.	
	"		2 O.Rs. proceeded on leave to U.K. 1 O.R. reported from leave in U.K.	
	16.7.18		A/Capt. Lee & A/Lt.Col. Nicklow detailed to attend as witnesses at Court of Enquiry to be held at H.Qrs. "B" Coy. 1/4th Leic Rifles, on 17.7.18.	
	17.7.18		Work on new gun positions commenced.	
	18.7.18		Sgt. Gowden struck off effective strength on proceeding to U.K. on commission.	
	19.7.18		1 O.R. reported from leave in U.K.	
	"		Gun positions completed at T.19.8.9.1. & T.26.a.8.4.	
	20.7.18		1 R.O. proceeded in advance to take over new area pending relief of Battery from line.	
	21.7.18		Battery relieved from line by 23rd T.M. Battery, & moved back to DURHAM CAMP, MONT ST ELOY.	
	22.7.18		Battery moved to BOIS D'OLHAIN & camped in wood there.	

156th Trench Mortar Battery.

Training Programme for week commencing 25th July 1918.

Hours of Parade	25th July	26th July	27th July	28th July	29th July	30th July	31st July
8 am to 8.30 am	Physical Training	Physical Training	Physical Training	Physical Training	Physical Training	Bayonet Fighting	Bayonet Fighting
8.45 am to 9.45 am	Battery Drill	Battery Drill and Fire Orders	Battery Drill and Fire Orders		Battery Drill and Fire Orders		Taking up positions and Fire Orders
9.45 am to 10.15 am	Lecture: Parts of Gun and N.C.O.s, Relief of Reliefs	Lecture: Dutiful Engagement before mounting Guns of Reliefs		Route March	Lecture: Assembling the Gun of Ammunition	Route March	Lecture: Ranging and Fire Effect, Fighting Fires
10.30 am to 11 am	Musketry Exercises	Musketry Exercises			Musketry Exercises		Musketry Exercises
1.30 pm to 2 pm	N.C.Os + No Ones Lecture: Duties of Mounting + Detachments Etc.	N.C.Os + No Ones Lecture: Ranging			N.C.Os + No Ones Lecture: Interpretation of Lighting and Tickling Etc.		N.C.Os + No Ones Lecture: Ranging

Michan Capt.
O.C. 156th T.M. Battery

WAR DIARY or INTELLIGENCE SUMMARY

156th M. Battery. Sheet No. 4

Army Form C. 2118.

Place	Date	Hour	Summary of Events and Information	Remarks and references to Appendices
BOIS D'OLHAIN	22.7.18		1 O.R. proceeded on leave to U.K.	
	23.7.18		L/Bdrs. Kerr & Enderdebrined of Lance Stripes.	
	24.7.18		Gun Drill. Battery paraded. Gnrs. Rae & Richmond promoted to rank of L/Bdr. & A/Sgt. Reed to Sgt.	
	25.7.18		Training as per programme. 1 Off. to Hospital. 2nd Lieut. W.A. Gilling & Gunners Hunt, Royal Scots, reported for duty.	
	26.7.18		Training as per programme.	
	27.7.18		do. do. do.	
	28.7.18		do. do. do. Divine Service.	
	"		L/Bdr. Shaw promoted to rank of H/Bdr.	
	29.7.18		Training as per programme. 1 Off. & 1 O.R. proceeded on leave to U.K. Lieut. W.N. Somerville takes over command of Battery during absence of Capt. Scott on leave to U.K. 1 O.R. returned from leave in U.K.	
	30.7.18		Battery marched to CLIFF CAMP, ECOIVRES.	
	31.7.18		O.C. Battery went round new sector of line.	

156th T.M. Battery

WAR DIARY or INTELLIGENCE SUMMARY

Army Form C. 2118.

Place	Date	Hour	Summary of Events and Information	Remarks and references to Appendices
Battery H.Q. B.26.d.4.2. BAILLEUL (2nd Edition) 1/20,000	3/4/18		Battery relieved 116th Canadian T.M. Battery in Right Brigade sector of line. Six guns in line, & two in reserve at Battery HQrs. Some H.E. & Gas Shelling at Battery Headquarters. Disposition of Guns in line :- No. 1. A.3.d.10.65. No. 4. B.22.c.40.35. " 2. A.3.a.90.30. " 5. B.22.a.90.15. " 3. B.24.b.45.25. " 6. B.16.a.50.50. Personnel of Battery at this date :- Officers Other Ranks 1. 11th Royal Scots. 11. 14th Royal Scots. 2. 11/7th Royal Scots. 14. 11/7th Royal Scots. 1. 1/8 H.L.I. Scottish Rifles 10. 1/7th Scottish Rifles. 11. 1/8th Scottish Rifles. Wm Farnsworth Lieut. O/C 156th T.M. Battery	

WAR DIARY
or
INTELLIGENCE SUMMARY

Confidential

War Diary
— of —
156th Trench Mortar Battery.

1st to 31st August, 1918.

Volume XIII

WAR DIARY or INTELLIGENCE SUMMARY

Army Form C. 2118.

156th T.M. Battery. Sheet No. 1.

Place	Date	Hour	Summary of Events and Information	Remarks and references to Appendices
Battery H.Qrs. B.26.b.y.2. BAILLEUL (2nd Edit.) 1/20,000.	1/8/18.		Disposition of Guns in line:- No. 1. H.3.d.10.65. No.4. B.22.a.40.35. (Two Guns in " 2. H.3.a.90.50. " 5. B.22.a.90.15. reserve at " 3. B.27.d.45.25. " 6. B.16.c.50.50. Battery H.Qrs.) Personnel of Battery at this date:- Officers. Other Ranks. 1. 1/4th Royal Scots. 11. 1/4th Royal Scots. 2. 1/7th Royal Scots. 14. 1/7th Royal Scots. 1. 1/8th Scottish Rifles. 10. 1/7th Scottish Rifles. 11. 1/8th Scottish Rifles.	
	1/8/18.		No.6 Gun Position & Ammunition, Etc, taken over by 154th T.M. Battery, and own Gun taken into reserve at Battery H.Qrs.	N/A
	"		Improvements to emplacements & cleaning of shells	
	"		1 O.R struck off Effective strength on being by days in Field Ambulance.	

156th T.M. Battery.

WAR DIARY
or
INTELLIGENCE SUMMARY.

Sheet No. 2.

Army Form C. 2118.

Place	Date	Hour	Summary of Events and Information	Remarks and references to Appendices
	2/8/18		Improvements to emplacements & cleaning of shells	140
	"		2 O.Rs. reported for duty from leave in U.K.	
	"	10.30AM	Slight hostile gas shelling in vicinity of Battery H.Qrs.	140
	3/9/18		Improvements to emplacements & cleaning ammunition	140
	4/9/18		do	140
	5/9/18		do	140
	6/9/18		1 O.R. proceeded on 14 days leave to U.K.	
			No.1 Gun position. Ammunition taken over by 173rd T.M. Battery. Own gun taken into reserve at Battery Hq.	140
			3 O.Rs. detailed to attend as witnesses at F.G.C.M. assembling at ROCLINCOURT at 10 am on 8/6/18	
			1 O.R. struck off effective strength as a deserter.	
			1 O.R. reported for duty from leave in U.K.	
	7/9/18		Preparing new position for 8 Guns on the line & cleaning ammunition.	140

152nd In Battery

Army Form C. 2118.

WAR DIARY
or
INTELLIGENCE SUMMARY.
Sheet No 3

(Erase heading not required.)

Instructions regarding War Diaries and Intelligence Summaries are contained in F.S. Regs., Part II. and the Staff Manual respectively. Title pages will be prepared in manuscript.

Place	Date	Hour	Summary of Events and Information	Remarks and references to Appendices
	8/9/18		Battery preserving on new positions in line obtaining ammunition	AS
	9/9/18		Four remounts num'd in line handed over to 172nd In Bay	AS
			10th June 14 days pay tribute 1 days pay under 8.13 for men stopping his leave to U.K. by 1 day.	
	10/9/18		Battery preserving on new positions in line obtaining Ammunition	AS
			1 O.R. struck off 1 O.R. taken on Effective Strength	
	11/9/18		Battery preserving in new positions in line	AS
			Battery arrangements	
			new position to Removing dumps nearer	
	12/9/18		to	AS
			1 O.R. admitted by Field Ambulance (sick)	
			4 of the new positions in the line occupied.	

WAR DIARY
or INTELLIGENCE SUMMARY.

Army Form C. 2118.

15th Dn Battery

Place	Date	Hour	Summary of Events and Information	Remarks and references to Appendices
	13/8/18		Shifting ammunition to the positions. Work proceeding on the other four finished sites to attain a minimum 3 f.b.m. at St Pol.	WD
	14/8/18		Shewing ammunition. Work proceeding on new position	WD
	15/8/18		Battery relieved from the line by the 157th Dn Battery. Marched to ECURIE & entrained for SAVY	WD
	16/8/18		Arrived at SAVY & marched to billets in BERLES. Capt Jno Scott reported for duty from 14 days leave in U.K.	WD
BERLES	17/8/18		Shewing guns & generally improving Sanitary arrangements etc.	WD
	18/8/18		Shewing guns. Parades 6.0 am till 8.30 am Physical drill 9 to 11 am. Gun drill. D.B. struck off the effective strength of this unit as from 19/8/18 on having 7 days in Field Ambulance.	WD

WAR DIARY or INTELLIGENCE SUMMARY.

Army Form C. 2118.

156" Mr Battery Sheet No. 5

Place	Date	Hour	Summary of Events and Information	Remarks and references to Appendices
BERLES	19/8/18		30% taken on Effective strength of the unit	N/A
			O.R. reported for duty from 14 days leave in U.K.	N/A
	19/8/18		Parade 8 am to 8.30 am. Officers hour.	
		9.45 am	13 12 midday Packing papers.	
		10.R	proceeded on 14 days leave to U.K.	N/A
	20/8/18		Battery marched in view of 19th R.I. to the Camps in BERNEVILLE	N/A
BERNEVILLE	21/8/18		Stayed overnight in Camp. To tomorrow proceed on 14 days leave to U.K.	N/A
	22/8/18		Took our Gun proceeded with Limber party reconnoitre ground previous to the attack	N/A
			Battery in horses at 10 pm. Journeyed to BLAIREVILLE	
BLAIREVILLE	23/8/18		Battery held in readiness to send four guns to the new line. This order was cancelled + Battery spent the day in carrying forward water for the attacking troops	N/A
	24/8/18		Battery resumed work of carrying water + ammunition transporting forward that same whelmed in Comps for muck gutter	N/A

Army Form C. 2118.

WAR DIARY
or
INTELLIGENCE SUMMARY.
(Erase heading not required.)

15th Gun Battery Sheet No 6.

Place	Date	Hour	Summary of Events and Information	Remarks and references to Appendices
FRANCE Edition 8d Local Sheet 51 B SW 1/20,000	24/8/18		Battery HQrs moved forward to S.2.b.6.2.	N/B
	25/8/18		Battery resumed work of carrying water & collecting butts, also two other cases at gun when others were received to put to guns into the line.	N/B
			2 Guns to 7th Royal Scots thence to 9th Ls Rifles. After several eons guns were hauled forward & put into position at N.32.b.5.7. & N.26.a.3.3. Remainder of battery carried ammunition to new positions.	
	26/8/18		Battery HQrs moved forward to M.35.a.9.5. Guns were placed under orders of Infantry.	N/B
			Battery HQrs moved forward to T.1.K.1.5. 10.9. to Kinkton (wounded 2026 Private KNR on keeps gun) Lewis moved forward to Battery concentrate at N.34.a.7.8. & later moved forward to	N/B
	27/8/18		16. N.36. central.	N/B
	28/8/18		Brigade returned – Battery moved back to Sunken Road M.35.c.2.7.	N/B

156th Dn Battery

WAR DIARY
or
INTELLIGENCE SUMMARY
(Erase heading not required.)

Army Form C. 2118.

Instructions regarding War Diaries and Intelligence Summaries are contained in F.S. Regs., Part II. and the Staff Manual respectively. Title pages will be prepared in manuscript.

Heut No. 7

Place	Date	Hour	Summary of Events and Information	Remarks and references to Appendices
M35 C.3.7	29.8.18		Battery resting	No
	30.8.18		do	No
U7 a.8.3	31.8.18		Battery moved into support line with brigade & took over from 168th 2M Battery	
FRANCE EDITION 8ab LOCAL SHEET 51 b.S.W 1/20,000.			Personnel of Battery at this date	No
			Officers Other Ranks	
			2 1/7th Bn The Royal Scots 11 1/4 U Bn The Royal Scots	
			1 16th " " " " 16 1/7th " " " " "	
			___ 10 1/9th " The Scottish Rifles	
			3 9 1/6th " do do	
			— 46	

M. Smith Capt.
Commdg 156th 2M Battery

Army Form C. 2118.

WAR DIARY
or
INTELLIGENCE SUMMARY.
(Erase heading not required.)

Confidential

War Diary

of

156th Trench Mortar Battery

1st to 30th September 1918

Volume XIV

WAR DIARY
INTELLIGENCE SUMMARY

Army Form C. 2118.

156th T.M. Battery

Sheet 51b S.W. Vol XIV

FRANCE
Edition 8a
(Local)
1/20,000

Place	Date	Hour	Summary of Events and Information	Remarks and references to Appendices
Battery HQM U.7.a.8.4.	1/9/18		O.C. Battery attended conference at Bde HQrs where orders were received that on the attacking battery would join 17th Royal Scots (Supporting Bn) in Gordon Reserve U.28.a. This was afterwards cancelled	N/O
	2/9/18		Battery moved to KNUCKLE AVENUE U.14.C.71 carrying four guns & ammunition. During forward armouries was arranged. At 2.30 pm orders were received to dispatch one section forward under 2/Lt M. Colquit picking up limber load of ammunition come early orders of O.C. 17th Royal Scots. Section proceeded to CROISILLES – BULLECOURT Road Ammunition dump was formed close to 17th R.S. HQrs at U.22.d. At 6 pm orders were received to dispatch remaining section to come under orders of O.C. 19th Scottish Rifles which was carried out. Ammunition dump was formed at KNUCKLE AVENUE QUEANT ROAD. Battery HQrs remained at Knuckle Avenue	N/S

136th T.M. Battery.

WAR DIARY
INTELLIGENCE SUMMARY

Sheet No. 2   Vol. XIV

Army Form C. 2118.

Place	Date	Hour	Summary of Events and Information	Remarks and references to Appendices
U14 C 7	3/9/18		Battery dug out moved up to U.30 d where Brigade concentrated	T/O
			TM B's proceeded on 14 days leave to U.K.	T/O
U.30 d	4/9/18		Day was spent in all	T/O
	5/9/18		Battery concentrated at 10 am (Resting)	T/O
	6/9/18		Resting	T/O
ST LEDGER	7/9/18		Battery moved to bivouac area close to ST LEDGER	T/O
"	8/9/18		Resting 10 R reported for duty from leave U.K.	T/O
"	9/9/18		Physical drill 8-30 to 9 am 10 am Bathing Parade	T/O
			2 ORs proceeded on 14 days leave to U.K.	
	10/9/18		Parades — 8.30 to 9 am Physical drill	T/O
			9.30 to 10 am Handling of arms	
			10.0 to 11 am Battery Order	
	11/9/18		do	T/O
			1 OR admitted to Field ambulance sick	
	12/9/18		Parades 8.30 to 9 am Physical drill 9.30 to 10 am Musketry 10 to 11 am Battery Drill	T/O
			Coys for 1 Capt. attended 7.9.16.18 as a member	

Army Form C. 2118.

WAR DIARY
or
INTELLIGENCE SUMMARY.
(Erase heading not required.)

16th Trench Mortar Battery

Sheet No. 3   Vol. XIV

Instructions regarding War Diaries and Intelligence Summaries are contained in F. S. Regs., Part II. and the Staff Manual respectively. Title pages will be prepared in manuscript.

Place	Date	Hour	Summary of Events and Information	Remarks and references to Appendices
ST LEDGER	1/9/18		Parade 8-30 a.m. Physical exercises	N/9
		9.30 to 10 a.m	Musketry	
		10 to 11 a.m	Battery drill	
	2/9/18		Parade 8.30 to 9 a.m. Physical Exercises	N/9
		9.30 to 10 a.m	Musketry (reading of message)	
		10 to 10.45 a.m	Battery drill with guns & fuse setters	
		10.45 to 11 a.m	Lecture Ranging.	
	5/9/18		2ORs warned for duty from leave in UK Rifle & SBR inspection at 10 a.m.	N/9
		10.30 a.m	Divine Service at Agnes Scottish Rifles	
			Battery attended Brigade parade where GOC presented Military Medal	
			to Bdr A.C. Kingham of this unit being a recipient	
	6/9/18		At 12.15 p.m. battery paraded off with Bde Hqrs to D1a25 where it took	N/9
			over from the 17th? 2 MB (Still in reserve)	
	7/9/18	9-30 a.m	Rifle inspection	N/9
			Lecture working Lewis & Bde Hqr. 2ORs proceeded on 14 days leave to UK	
D1a25		12 noon	Listening guns 10 a.m. 5 12 noon	

156th A.M. Battery.

WAR DIARY or INTELLIGENCE SUMMARY

Army Form C. 2118.

Vol XIV
Sheet No. 4.

Place	Date	Hour	Summary of Events and Information	Remarks and references to Appendices
D.1.a 2.5	18/9/18		Rifle inspection 9.30 am. Inspection of guns 10.30 am. N.C.O. meeting struck off effective strength as from 16/9/18 being ordered a Medical Board by War Office. 2/Lt. Araxes to attend Divisional Signalling board at BOISLEUX AU MONT. Lt Ewen working party to Div Sgt.	N/O
	19/9/18		Moved to new area at D.15 (see [illegible])	N/O
D.15	20/9/18		O.C. Battery Section officer wrote line. Returned 156th 2nd W. Battery at E.19.a.8.8. 6 Guns in the line. 1/2 Mission taken on effective strength.	N/O
Hyp E.9 a 88	21/9/18		11 O.R. admitted to Field Ambulance Sect N.Y.D. No 2 Section fired 50 rounds return enemy counter attacks with good result. 1 O.R. slightly wounded.	N/O
	22/9/18		Ammunition taken forward from Bin Dump to guns in line by Infantry, enemy forces at enemy working party shooting No fire to Infantry our occupants. 2 O.Rs reported for duty from 14 days leave in UK.	N/O

WAR DIARY or INTELLIGENCE SUMMARY

Army Form C. 2118.

156th T.M. Battery   Vol XIV   Sheet No. 5

Place	Date	Hour	Summary of Events and Information	Remarks and references to Appendices
Hqrs E.19.a.8.8.	23/9/18		Ammunition taken forward from Bde Dumps to forward sections	N/A
	24/9/18		Relieved by 155th T.M. Battery & moved into reserve at D.14.a.9.6. In reserve (Resting). Battery Batmen reported for duty with battery.	N/A
	25/9/18		O.C. Battery visited area selected for Bde advanced dump. 2 O.Rs. admitted to Field Ambulance (Sick N.Y.D.)	N/A
	26/9/18		Battery moved to our Bde Advanced Dump at D.30.b.1.4.	N/A
D.30.b.1.4	27/9/18		Supplied infantry with ammunition partie from advanced dump.	N/A
	28/9/18		Battery engaged on Salvage Work. (In Reserve)	N/A
	29/9/18		do do	N/A
	29/9/18		2 O.Rs. returned to duty from Field Ambulance.	N/A
	30/9/18		11 O.Rs. (10 Effective & 1 Attached) struck off strength. (Wounded Gas) In Reserve (Resting).	N/A

WAR DIARY
INTELLIGENCE SUMMARY

156th T.M. Battery. Sheet No. 6. Vol XIV

Place	Date	Hour	Summary of Events and Information	Remarks
	30/9/18		Personnel of Battery at this date:-	
			Officers.	
			1. 1/4th Royal Scotts.	
			2. 1/4th Royal Scotts.	
			3.	
			Other Ranks.	
			13. 1/4th Royal Scots.	N.S.
			10. 1/4th Royal Scots.	
			6. 1/4th Scottish Rifles	
			6. 1/8th Scottish Rifles	
			35.	
			G. Scott Capt.	
			Comndg. 156th T.M. Battery.	

Army Form C. 2118.

WAR DIARY
or
INTELLIGENCE SUMMARY.
(Erase heading not required.)

Original

Confidential

War Diary
—of—
156th Trench Mortar Battery
1st to 31st October 1916.

Volume XV

Army Form C. 2118.

WAR DIARY
or
INTELLIGENCE SUMMARY.
(Erase heading not required.)

156th A.M. Battery. Sheet No. 1   Vol. XV

Place	Date	Hour	Summary of Events and Information	Remarks and references to Appendices
Battery HQrs	1/10/18		Battery moved into reserve at L 3 c 1-7	N/O
L 3 c 1-7			20 OR reported for duty from leave in UK	N/O
Sheet 57c	2/10/18		Resting	N/O
NE	3/10/18		Furnished fatigue parties for Bakers	
	4/10/18		Resting	N/O
			1 OR (absent without leave) reported for duty.	N/O
	5/10/18		Battery collected salvage in area allied.	
	6/10/18		Battery reinforcements marched to bivouac area near Luges	N/O
			Battery staying there the night.	
	7/10/18		Marched to Racefield retaining for TINQUES. Marched	N/O
			from TINQUES to billets in IZEL-LES-HAMEAUX.	
IZEL-LES-HAMEAUX	8/10/18		Guns Ammunition arrived afternoon	N/O
	9/10/18		Battery Resting during the forenoon. 1 OR proceeded on leave to UK.	N/O
	10/10/18		do	N/O
	11/10/18		do	N/O

WAR DIARY or INTELLIGENCE SUMMARY

156th Tm Battery

Army Form C. 2118.

Sheet No 2.

Place	Date	Hour	Summary of Events and Information	Remarks and references to Appendices
IZEL-LES-HAMEAUX	12/6/18		Parade during forenoon. Bathing & disinfecting parades. 1 OR proceeded on leave to U.K.	W/O
	13/6/18		Divine Service. 22 ORs taken on strength of battery as from the 12th Oct 1918	W/O
	14/6/18		Parades during forenoon. 3 NCOs & 6 Men assembled at MAIZIERES at 10 am for the funeral of No 302764 Pte L Kennedy 17th R.S. att. 156th Tm Battery. 1 OR & 1 Driver detailed to act as pallbearers.	W/O
	15/6/18		Parades during forenoon. Gas lecture with 4th R.S.L carried out. Enchoir exercises with 17th R.S.L 1 OR admitted to 2 Ambulance (Sick).	W/O
	16/6/18		do. Battery carried out tactical scheme with 17th Lan Rif. & 17th R.S.	16/8
	17/6/18		do 1 OR admitted to 2 Ambulance (Sick) 1 OR returned for duty from hospital	W/O

Army Form C. 2118.

WAR DIARY
or
INTELLIGENCE SUMMARY.
(Erase heading not required.)

16 A.A. M. Battery

Instructions regarding War Diaries and Intelligence Summaries are contained in F.S. Regs., Part II. and the Staff Manual respectively. Title pages Sheet No 3 ___Vol XV___ will be prepared in manuscript.

Place	Date	Hour	Summary of Events and Information	Remarks and references to Appendices
IZEL-LES-HAMEAUX	18/6/18		Parades during forenoon. 1 section (2 guns) carried out machine scheme with 7th L.R.B. S.B.R. etc.	
			1 O.R. proceeded on 14 days leave to U.K.	
			No 300706 St L Hervey of this battery tried by F.G.C.M. on the charge of absence without leave was sentenced to one years imprisonment with hard labour. Sentence commuted to 90 days F.P. No 1 by convening officer	N/A
	19/6/18		Marched to CHATEAU DE LA HAIE & stayed overnight	N/A
	20/6/18		1 O.R. proceeded on 14 days leave to U.K.	
			Marched to BILLY MONTIGNY. Billets in evacuated houses	N/A
			1 O.R. proceeded on 14 days leave to U.K.	
AUBY 36.c.4.3 Sheet 44a	21/6/18		Marched to AUBY. Billeted in evacuated houses	N/A
			1 O.R. admitted to F. Ambulance (sick)	
	22/6/18		Rifle inspection, general cleaning up	
			do	
	23/6/18		1 O.R. struck off effective strength as from 20/6/18	N/A

WAR DIARY or INTELLIGENCE SUMMARY

Army Form C. 2118.

13th Trench Mortar Battery

Vol XI

(Erase heading not required.)

Place	Date	Hour	Summary of Events and Information	Remarks and references to Appendices
AUBY	21/8/18		Battery marched to COUTICHES. Capt Scott returned to OR	
			proceeded to attend course at GHQ Light Mortar School	A/9
LE TOUQUET			OR proceed on leave to UK.	
COUTICHES	23/8/18		Lt A.C. Butter took over command of battery as from 24/8/18 in absence of Capt. Scott at 2/c Coutie.	A/9
M2 a 2.3 Sheet 44			Training 0900 to 1300. Road work 1400 to 1600	
	26/8/18		OR struck off effective strength as from 24/8/18	A/9
	27/8/18		Training 0900 to 1200. Road work 1400 to 1600.	A/9
			Marched to LECELLES a break-down evacuated horses	
			to R proceeded on horse transport.	
LECELLES			OR admitted to Ambulance (sick) 27/8/18 struck off effective strength as from 28/8/18	
	28/8/18	0500	Billets shelled. Horses badly damaged. Marched to MONT ROY (J27 d 2.3 Batty H.Q.) Two guns in the line with 17th R.S.	A/9

WAR DIARY or INTELLIGENCE SUMMARY

150th T.M. Battery   Sheet No. 5   Vol XV   Army Form C. 2118.

Place	Date	Hour	Summary of Events and Information	Remarks and references to Appendices
T33 A9.9	29/10/18	0900	Rifle Instruction. Battery moved to T33 a.9.9	N/A
Sheet 44	30/10/18		Training :- 1000 to 1200 Gun drill	N/A
44.0.0		0900	do. Mortar Instruction	
	31/10/18	0900	Rifle Instruction Training - 1000 to 1200 do. Bathing Parade at H.Q.s. J.W.C.Rfs 1 O.R. returned for duty on return from leave in U.K.	
			Lt A Trotter taken on effective strength as from 21-10-18	N/A
			Personnel of Battery at this date.	
			Officers Other Ranks	
			2 1/4th Royal Scots 18 1/4th Royal Scots	
			2 1/7th Royal Scots 14 1/7th Royal Scots	
			— 9 1/7th Scottish Rifles	
			4 7 1/8th Scottish Rifles	
			51	

A Trotter Lieut
Commdg 152nd T.M. Battery.

Army Form C. 2118.

WAR DIARY
or
INTELLIGENCE SUMMARY.
(Erase heading not required.)

Original

Confidential

War Diary
of
156th Trench Mortar Battery

1st to 31st December, 1918

Volume XVII

156th M. Battery.

WAR DIARY or ~~INTELLIGENCE SUMMARY~~

Army Form C. 2118.

Sheet No. 1

Place	Date	Hour	Summary of Events and Information	Remarks and references to Appendices
THORICOURT	1/12/18		Rifle and billet inspections. Cleaning equipment, etc.	a/s
	2/12/18		Physical training. Battery Drill. Taking up positions. Squad Drill and Handling of Arms.	a/s
	3/12/18		Lecture. Ranging.	a/s
	"		Physical training. Battery Drill. Handling of Arms. Lecture. 1 O.R. reported for duty from leave in U.K.	a/s
	4/12/18		Physical training. Battery Drill. Handling of Arms. Lecture.	a/s
	5/12/18		Route March. Lieut. H. Lotter reported for duty from leave in U.K.	a/s
	6/12/18		Physical training. Battery Drill. Gun mounting. Handling of Arms.	a/s
	7/12/18		Do. Digging Positions & Gun mounting. Battery Drill.	a/s
	8/12/18		Divine Service. 4 O.Rs. reported for duty from leave in U.K.	a/s
	9/12/18		Training as per programme.	a/s
	10/12/18		Do. 6 O.Rs. proceeded to spend 24	a/s
	11/12/18		Do. 2 6 O.Rs. reported from D.A.C.	a/s
	12/12/18		Do. 6 O.Rs. proceeded to D.A.C. for like purpose. 1 O.R. proceeded on leave in U.K.	a/s

156th M. Battery.

WAR DIARY

Army Form C. 2118.

Sheet No. 2

Place	Date	Hour	Summary of Events and Information	Remarks and references to Appendices
THORICOURT	13/12/18		Brigade inspected by Divisional Commander.	act
	14/12/18		Training as per programme.	act
	15/12/18		Divine Service. 1 Officer and 1 O.R. returned for duty from leave in U.K.	act
	16/12/18		Battery moved to HUBERMONT.	act
HUBERMONT	17/12/18		Rifle and Billet Inspections. Cleaning of equipment, etc.	act
	18/12/18		Training as per programme.	act
	19/12/18		Do	act
	20/12/18		Do	act
	21/12/18		Do 1 O.R. reported for duty from leave in U.K.	act
	22/12/18		Divine Service.	act
	23/12/18		Training as per programme.	act
	24/12/18		Do	act
	25/12/18		Christmas Day. (Holiday).	act
	26/12/18		Training as per programme.	act
	27/12/18		Do 1 Officer proceeded on leave in U.K.	act

156th M. Battery.

WAR DIARY
or
INTELLIGENCE SUMMARY

Army Form C. 2118.

Sheet No. 3

Place	Date	Hour	Summary of Events and Information	Remarks and references to Appendices
HUBERMONT	28/12/18		Training as per programme. Capt. Jas. Scott detailed as member of G.C.M. assembling at H.Q'rs 6th H.A.G.	act.
	29/12/18		28th Decr. '18. at 1000. Divine Service. 1 O.R. admitted to Field Amb.	act.
	30/12/18		Ambulance (sick). Training as per programme. 1 Officer and 1 O.R. admitted to Hospital (Sick)	act.
	31/12/18		Training as per programme. 1 O.R. struck off effective strength	act.
	31/12/18		Personnel of Battery at this date:— Officers Other Ranks 2 114th Royal Scots 17 114th Royal Scots 2 117th Lovats Scouts 14 117th Lovats Scouts — 118th Lovats Rifles 8 118th Lovats Rifles — 17 46	act.

Ela. Scott Capt.
Comdg. 156th M. Battery.

156th Trench Mortar Battery.

Training Programme for week ending Saturday 14th December, 1918.

Hours of Parade.	Monday. 9th.	Tuesday. 10th.	Wednesday. 11th.	Thursday. 12th.	Friday. 13th.	Saturday. 14th.
0830 to 1130.	Route March L'ERSE— CHAUSSIÉ— LOUVIGNIES. Starts at 0900.	Physical Training Tactical Scheme.	Physical Training Battery Drill. Squad Drill. Handling of Arms	Physical Training Tactical Scheme.	Route March FOULENG.— GONDREGNIES— SILLY. Starts at 0900.	Physical Training Battery Drill Musketry

M. Leo Capt.
O.C. 156th T.M. Battery.

156th Trench Mortar Battery.

Training Programme for week ending Saturday, 21st December 1918.

Hour of Parade.	Monday. 16th.	Tuesday. 17th.	Wednesday. 18th.	Thursday. 19th.	Friday. 20th.	Saturday. 21st.
0830 to 1130.	Move to New Area.	Cleaning Up & Inspection.	Physical Training. Battery Drill. Musketry.	Physical Training. Battery Drill. Handling of Arms.	Route March. Route: CHAUSSEE N.D. LOUVIGNIES. Starts at 0900.	Physical Training. Battery Drill. Musketry.

Lieut Capt.
O/c 156th T.M. Battery.

156th Trench Mortar Battery.

Training Programme for week ending Saturday, 28th Decr. 1918.

Hours of Parade.	Monday. 23rd.	Tuesday. 24th.	Wednesday. 25th.	Thursday. 26th.	Friday. 27th.	Saturday. 28th.
0830 to 1130.	Physical Training. Battery Drill. Lecture.	Physical Training. Squad Drill. Musketry of Arms. Musketry.	Physical Training. Battery Drill. Bayonet Fighting.	Route March. Route:- GAILLY. Starts at 0900.	Tactical Scheme	Physical Training. Squad Drill. Musketry of Arms. Bayonet Fighting.

Michael Capt.
O/C 156th T.M. Battery.

156 H.S. Trench Mortar Battery.

Training Programme week beginning Saturday. 30th Aug. 1919.

	Saturday 30th.	Sunday 31st.	Monday 1st.	Tuesday 2nd.	Wednesday 3rd.	Thursday 4th.
Troops of Parade						
08.30	Physical training.	Physical training.	Church parade.	Route march.	Repair defects.	Physical training.
	Squad drill.	Battery drill.				Squad drill.
13.30	Games.	Games.	Holiday.	MONTIGNIES-LES-LENS Shoot at 0900	Shoot at 0900	Games. Sports.

Ernest McCalt
Capt.
O/C. 156 H.S.T.M. Battery.

Army Form C. 2118.

WAR DIARY
or
INTELLIGENCE SUMMARY.
(Erase heading not required.)

Original

Confidential

War Diary
of
156th Trench Mortar Battery.
1st to 31st January, 1919.

Volume XVIII.

156th A.M. Battery.

WAR DIARY
or
INTELLIGENCE SUMMARY.

Army Form C. 2118.

Place	Date	Hour	Summary of Events and Information	Remarks and references to Appendices
HUBERMONT.	1/1/19		New Year's Day. (Holiday)	
	2/1/19		Training as per programme.	
	3/1/19		Do.	
	4/1/19		Do.	
	"		Two O/Rs. struck off effective strength on being admitted to Hospital (sick).	
	6/1/19		Training as per programme.	
	7/1/19		Do.	
	8/1/19		Do.	} A.C.I.
			Brigade Ceremonial Parade at MONTIGNIES-LEZ-LENS.	
	9/1/19		Training as per programme.	
	10/1/19		Do.	
	11/1/19		Do.	} A.C.I.

WAR DIARY

Army Form C. 2118.

156th D.M. Battery.

Intelligence Summary.
(Erase heading not required.)

Sheet No. 2

Place	Date	Hour	Summary of Events and Information	Remarks and references to Appendices
HUBERMONT	13/1/19		Training as per programme.	
"	"		Two O.R.s proceeded on short leave in BRUSSELS.	
"	14/1/19		Three O.R.s proceeded for demobilization.	
"	"		Training as per programme.	
"	"		One Offr. proceeded for demobilization.	
"	15/1/19		Training as per programme.	
"	"		Two O.R.s returned from short leave in BRUSSELS.	
"	16/1/19		Training as per programme.	
"	"		Lieut. V. J. Ogilvy reported for duty on return from leave in U.K.	
"	17/1/19		Training as per programme.	
"	18/1/19		Lieut. W.A. Hilliard struck off effective strength as being evacuated sick - the Mich. 11/1/19.	a.s.
"	"		One O.R. taken on effective strength. (From Hopkins)	

WAR DIARY or **INTELLIGENCE SUMMARY**

Army Form C. 2118.

156th M. Battery.

Sheet No. 3

Place	Date	Hour	Summary of Events and Information	Remarks
HUBERMONT.	20/1/19		Training as per programme.	
"	21/1/19		Escort of one NCO and one Private proceeded to A.P.M. 5th Army, NAMUR, to take over into custody Pte. Murphy J, 18th Leo. Rifles (Deserter). One O/R proceeded for demobilization.	
"	22/1/19		Training as per programme. Two O/Rs proceeded for demobilization.	
"	23/1/19		Training as per programme. Do.	
"			Escort returned from NAMUR with Pte. Murphy J. 18th Leo. Rifles (Deserter). Two O/Rs (Signallers) taken on attached strength.	
"	24/1/19		Training as per programme. Do.	

ns 158/M T.M. Battery

WAR DIARY
INTELLIGENCE SUMMARY
Sheet No 4

Army Form C. 2118.

Place	Date	Hour	Summary of Events and Information	Remarks and references to Appendices
HUBERMONT	25/1/19		Training as per Programme	acy.
"	26/1/19	10 P.	reported from leave in U.K.	acy.
		2 O.R.	proceeded on short leave to Brussels	
"	27/1/19		Capt J. Scott proceeded to U.K. for demobilization	acy.
			2 Lieut P.C. Tasker assumed command of Battery	
			Training as per Programme	
"	28/1/19		Training as per Programme	acy.
			1 O.R. proceeded to U.K. for demobilization	
			1 O.R. reported for duty from Hospital	
"	29/1/19		Training as per programme	acy
"	30/1/19		do do do do	acy
"	31/1/19		do do do	acy
			Personnel of Battery at this date:-	
			Other Ranks:-	
			14 - 1/5th Royal Scots	
			10 - 1/7th " "	
			6 - 1/8th Scot. Rifles	
			4 - 1/8th " "	
			34	
			Officers	
			2 - 1/4 Royal Scots	
			2	a/See the Annual R. 158 T.M. 13/4

Army Form C. 2118.

WAR DIARY
or
INTELLIGENCE SUMMARY.
(Erase heading not required.)

Confidential

War Diary
of
the 156th Trench Mortar Battery
1st to 10th February, 1919.

Volume XIX

Army Form C. 2118.

156th Trench Mortar Battery

WAR DIARY
or
INTELLIGENCE SUMMARY.
(Erase heading not required.)

Instructions regarding War Diaries and Intelligence Summaries are contained in F.S. Regs., Part II. and the Staff Manual respectively. Title pages will be prepared in manuscript.

Place	Date	Hour	Summary of Events and Information	Remarks and references to Appendices
HUBERMONT.	1-2-19		Training as per programme.	
"	2-2-19		Divine Service.	
"	3-2-19		Training as per programme. One O.R. proceeded for demobilisation.	
"	4-2-19		Training as per programme. One O.R. proceeded for demobilisation.	
"	5-2-19		Training as per programme. One O.R. proceeded on short leave to Bruxelles.	
"	6-2-19		Training as per programme.	
"	7-2-19		Training as per programme. 2 O.R'S proceeded for demobilisation.	
"	8-2-19		Training as per programme. 1 O.R. returned from leave in Bruxelles.	
"	9-2-19		Divine Service. 1 Officer proceeded for demobilisation.	
"	10-2-19		The 156th Light Trench Mortar Battery is reduced to Cadre of 1 man.	

N.J.O. g.d.g.d. Lieut
O/C 156 T.M.B.

www.ingramcontent.com/pod-product-compliance
Lightning Source LLC
Chambersburg PA
CBHW081450160426
43193CB00013B/2434